L I F E W A Y S

The Huron

970.3
Bial

R A Y M O N D   B I A L

BENCHMARK BOOKS

MARSHALL CAVENDISH
NEW YORK

SERIES CONSULTANT: JOHN BIERHORST

ACKNOWLEDGMENTS

This book would not have been possible without the generous help of a number of individuals and organizations that have devoted themselves to preserving the culture of the Huron. I would like especially to thank Mary Mandley at Sainte-Marie among the Hurons and Jamie Hunter at the Huron Indian Village for their gracious hospitality, including permission to make photographs at these wonderful sites in Midland, Ontario. I would also like to acknowledge the kind assistance of the National Archives, the Library of Congress, and the Philbrook Museum for providing a number of illustrations.

As always, I am very much indebted to Kate Nunn and Doug Sanders for guiding this book through to completion and to John Bierhorst for his careful review of the manuscript. I would like to thank my wife, Linda, and my children, Anna, Sarah, and Luke, especially for their help during our trip to Huronia in the forests and lakes of Ontario to make photographs for this book.

Benchmarks Books
Marshall Cavendish Corporation
99 White Plains Road, Tarrytown, New York 10591-9001
Text copyright © 2001 by Raymond Bial
Map copyright © 2001 by the Marshall Cavendish Corporation
Map by Rodica Prato

Library of Congress Cataloging-in-Publication Data
Bial, Raymond.
The Huron / Raymond Bial.
p. cm. — (Lifeways)
Includes bibliographical references and index.
Summary: Discusses the history, culture, social structure, beliefs, and customs of the Huron people, also known as the Wyandot.
ISBN 0-7614-0940-8
1. Wyandot Indians—History—Juvenile literature. 2. Wyandot Indians—Social life and customs—Juvenile literature. [1. Wyandot Indians. 2. Indians of North America.] I.Title.
E99.H9B43 2001 973.04'9755—dc21 99-049261
Printed in Italy
6 5 4 3 2 1

Cover photos: Raymond Bial

The photographs in this book are used by permission and through the courtesy of:
Linda Sioui: 1, 34, 38-39, 45, 47, 55, 61, 67, 76-77, 78, 93. Raymond Bial: 6, 8-9, 12, 15, 17, 21, 22, 25, 26-27, 28, 29, 30, 31, 32, 37, 41, 42, 48, 52, 57, 64, 65, 66, 70, 73, 81, 85, 86, 88-89, 90, 103, 104-105, 109, 112-113. Canadian Museum of Civilization: 50-51. National Gallery of Canada, Ottawa: 95, 96. National Archives of Canada: PA 42596, 99; PA135187, 100; PA 178653, 106-107; PA 124103, 117.

This book is respectfully dedicated to the staff at Sainte-Marie among the Hurons and the Huron Indian Village, whose idealism and hard work are helping to keep alive the spirit of the Huron.

Contents

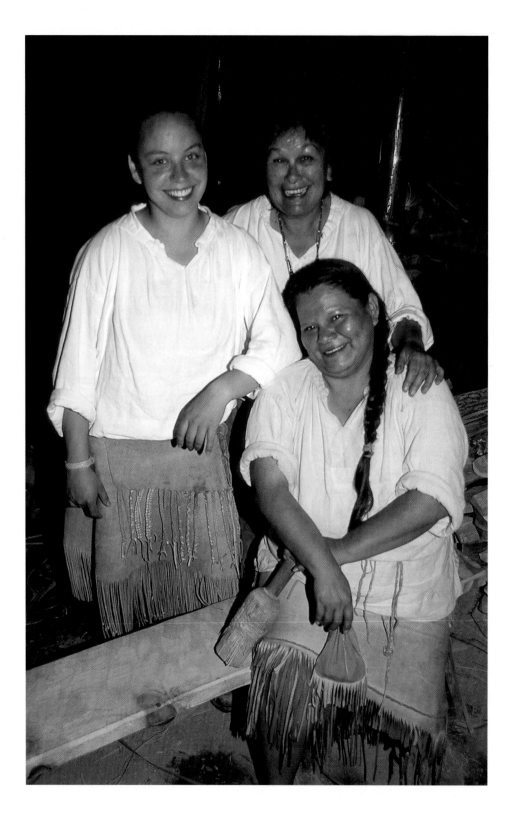

Author's Note

At THE DAWN OF THE TWENTIETH CENTURY, NATIVE Americans were thought to be a vanishing race. However, despite four hundred years of warfare, deprivation, and disease, American Indians have not gone away. Countless thousands have lost their lives, but over the course of this century the populations of native tribes have grown tremendously. Even as American Indians struggle to adapt to modern Western life, they have also kept the flame of their traditions alive—the language, religion, stories, and the everyday ways of life. An exhilarating renaissance in Native American culture is now sweeping the nation from coast to coast.

The Lifeways books depict the social and cultural life of the major nations, from the early history of native peoples in North America to their present-day struggles for survival and dignity. Historical and contemporary photographs of traditional subjects, as well as period illustrations, are blended throughout each book so that readers may gain a sense of family life in a tipi, a hogan, or a longhouse.

No single book can comprehensively portray the intricate and varied lifeways of an entire tribe, or nation. I only hope that young people will come away with a deeper appreciation for the rich tapestry of Indian culture—both then and now—and a keen desire to learn more about these first Americans.

1. Origins

For centuries, the Huron lived in the south of Canada not far from the rocky shores of Georgian Bay.

As they explored North America, the French encountered many native tribes, including an Iroquoian-speaking people whom they called *Huron*. They first met the Huron (HYUR-ahn), who called themselves Wendat, in 1609. The French found a thriving people living in villages scattered over a peninsula of rolling hills between Georgian Bay and Lake Simcoe, in what is now southern Ontario. Known as Wendake (Wen-DAH-kee), meaning "Land of the Wendat," and later as Huronia, this was a region of forests and lakes where men hunted and caught fish in abundance. The Huron were united in a political league, or confederacy, of four distinct nations. Within each nation, the Huron lived in fortified villages and in smaller villages and hamlets.

For hundreds of years, the Huron had prospered as farmers, growing corn, beans, and squash in clearings near their longhouses. As their harvests became more bountiful, they were able to sustain more people and began to form larger villages. Although settled as farmers, the Huron had to move when the light, sandy soil became exhausted—every ten to twenty years. They also traded surplus corn and other goods with the Algonquian hunters of the north. As their population increased, the Huron engaged in long-distance trade with their friends and organized warfare against their enemies.

The Huron enjoyed a strong alliance and a stable society, as well as a rich cultural life. Here is a version of the creation story they told over many generations, as people gathered around the longhouse fire.

The Creation Story

Many years ago, when there was only air and water, a woman named Aataentsic (ah-TANT-sik) lived in the Sky World. There were forests, lakes, rivers, and fields in the Sky World, and people lived there as they do now upon the earth. However, one day, Aataentsic fell through a great hole in the Sky World and tumbled downward through the air.

No one is certain why Aataentsic fell from the Sky World. Some people say she was hoeing in her cornfield and saw a bear. When her dog pursued the lumbering bear, Aataentsic went after her beloved pet. By accident, the bear stumbled and plunged into the hole, followed by the dog. Aataentsic crept to the edge of the hole and when she could see neither the bear nor the dog, she jumped into the abyss. Others say that her husband, who was very ill, dreamed that if he ate the fruit of a certain tree he would be cured. To reach the fruit, Aataentsic cut down the tree, but at the first swing of her ax, the tree split and crashed through the floor of the Sky World, leaving a chasm. Aataentsic told her husband what had happened. She then returned to the gaping hole and threw herself after the tree.

Aataentsic was heavy with child when she tumbled from the Sky World. A flock of swans recognized her plight and glided under her. Flying wing tip to wing tip, they made a feathery raft for her. However, there was no land on which they could set her down—only water below in which fish and other creatures swam. Aataentsic could neither fly nor swim for very long, and the swans did not know

*T*urtles and other wild creatures inhabit the swamps and marshes where the Huron came to make their home.

what to do with her. Finally, Turtle rose to the surface and called upon Beaver and all the other animals of the water. "Dive to the bottom and bring up soil," Beaver instructed. "Place the soil on my back." The animals did so, and an island grew on Turtle's back.

The swans gently placed Aataentsic on this island, and there she made her home. In time, she gave birth to two sons, Tawiscaron (da-WIS-ga-ron) and Youskeha (you-SKE-ha). As they grew up, however, the two brothers fought—Youskeha wielding the horns of a stag and Tawiscaron using the fruits of the wild rosebush as a weapon. On one occasion, Youskeha struck his brother so hard that his blood flowed over the land. Flint sprang up from the blood, and in the language of the Huron, this stone—which they chipped into points for arrows and spears—came to be called *tawiscara* in honor of the wounded brother.

Both brothers ruled over the earth as gods, wielding great power, yet acting as opposing forces. Youskeha often helped the people to have a better life, while his brother, Tawiscaron, became spiteful and brought only sorrow and death.

THOUSANDS OF YEARS AGO, THE ANCESTORS OF THE HURON AND OTHER Native Americans, journeyed over a strip of land that once linked Siberia and Alaska. Following the herds of shaggy bison and other wild animals, wandering bands spread south and eastward over the continent of North America. Eventually, about A.D. 500, the Huron settled in eastern Canada in what is now southern Ontario. Their name is derived from the French *hure*, meaning "boar." The term may refer to a hairstyle worn by some of the men—popularly known today as a Mohawk—in which the head is shaved except for a brushlike ridge along the center of the scalp. They called themselves *Wendat*, or *Ouendat*, meaning "Islanders" or "Dwellers on a Peninsula." The name may have come from their belief that the earth was a great island carried on the back of a turtle.

For the next five hundred years, in what became known as the pre-Iroquoian period, the Huron lived by hunting, fishing, and gathering. Around A.D. 1000, in the early Iroquoian period, they learned to raise corn. The additional food allowed people to gather in palisaded villages, where they lived in longhouses. Beginning about A.D. 1300, in the middle-Iroquoian period, the Huron began to plant sunflowers not only as a food but also for their oil. About a century later, in the late-Iroquoian period, they first cultivated beans and squash as crops. During this time, warfare escalated among the native peoples of the region, and the Hurons began to locate their villages closer together to better defend themselves.

This military cooperation led to the formation of a formal alliance, when four tribes known as the Attignawantan (Bear People), Attigneenongnahac (Cord People), Tahontaenrat (Deer People), and Arendahronon (Rock People) established the Huron League, possibly in the early 1500s. Within a century, the alliance had grown to include between 20,000 and 45,000 members living in sixteen to twenty-five villages, each with about 2,000 inhabitants. This powerful union enabled the Huron to dominate a swath of fertile land,

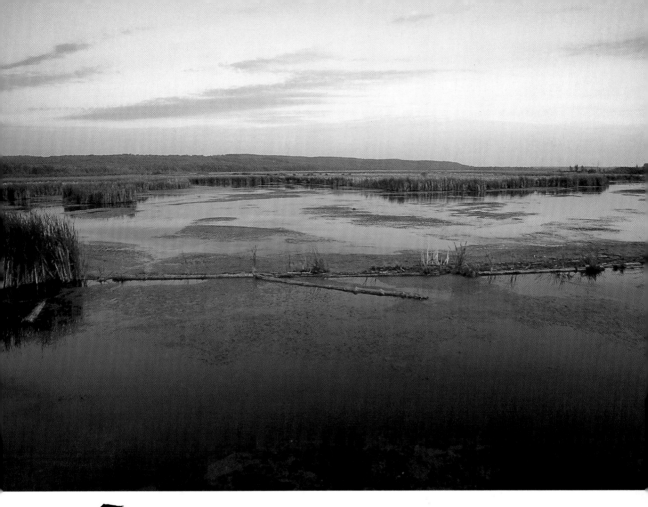

*T*he forests and fields of the Huron homeland were dotted with lakes and marshes teeming with wildlife.

about twenty miles long and thirty-five miles wide between Georgian Bay and Lake Simcoe, the area that became known as Huronia.

It was once believed that the Huron settled in this northern region to avoid the Iroquois, who lived in what is now upstate New York. Although the Iroquoian-speaking Hurons shared a similar language and customs with the Iroquois, including living in longhouses, they often warred with their neighbors to the south. Yet, despite the bitterly cold winters, the geography of Huronia also suited the people. The light soils could be easily worked, and Huronia was nearly sur-rounded by water. People caught fish in abundance throughout the year. Yet it was the location at the southern edge of the Canadian Shield, a bleak, rocky plain stretching to the Arctic, that became pivotal for trade. Here, too, were the only suitable canoe routes to the north. Algonquian hunters who wandered the north country exchanged furs and hides and dried meat and fish for nuggets of copper, which the Huron acquired by trade with peoples living to the west at Sault Sainte Marie and Lake Superior. The Algonquians also needed stores of corn to get through the winter, along with tobacco and other goods, which the Huron could provide for them.

When Jacques Cartier, a French explorer, encountered Iroquoian-speaking people near the present-day cities of Montreal and Quebec in the mid-1500s, the Huron were living primarily by farming, hunting, and fishing—as they had for several hundred years. In 1609, the Huron established friendly relations with French explorer Samuel de Champlain, after which they became the most active traders of all the native peoples in what became known as New France. They adeptly served as middlemen between the French and the native peoples of the Great Lakes region in a growing interna-tional trade in furs, notably beaver pelts.

Yet from the moment the Huron came into contact with the French, their way of life began to change. French explorers, traders, and missionaries arrived in Huronia over the next forty years and gradually formed a complex and ultimately destructive relationship with the native people. The Huron prospered as traders, yet they also became dependent on European goods. They strongly resisted the zealous attempts of Jesuit missionaries to save their souls, but the French also brought European diseases, notably measles and smallpox, against which the Huron had no resistance. Starting in the early 1630s, thousands of people died; entire villages within the confederacy perished. Many survivors, noting that the French did not succumb to these maladies, converted to Christianity, leading to bitter conflict with those who steadfastly embraced traditional beliefs.

When French traders and trappers came to Canada, they paddled rivers that led through the deep forests surrounding the Huron homeland.

Inset map labels:
Georgian Bay
Gahendoe Island
Wendake
Lake Simcoe

Ile d'Orleans
Quebec

HURONIA
until 1650

James Bay

CANADA

QUEBEC

ONTARIO

Quebec

MAINE

Lake Superior

St. Lawrence River

Montreal

MICHIGAN

Lake Huron

Georgian Bay

WISCONSIN

Wendake

Lake Ontario

Lake Michigan

Iroquois

NEW YORK

MICHIGAN

ILLINOIS

INDIANA

OHIO

Lake Erie

PENNSYLVANIA

ATLANTIC
OCEAN

This map shows the land of the Huron, just south of Georgian Bay in what is
now the province of Ontario.

The French provided written accounts of the Huron way of life in three documents: Samuel de Champlain's account of his winter in Huronia (1615–1616), Gabriel Sagard-Théobat's account of his winter sojourn (1623–1624), and the *Jesuit Relations* written during the years 1634 to 1650. The *Jesuit Relations* were annual reports written by Catholic missionaries of the Jesuit order, who were fervently attempting to convert the Huron. One of the best-known Jesuit missionaries was Father Jean de Brébeuf.

This became a tragic period, lasting barely a half-century, in which French and Huron alike struggled for survival through the deep snow and dark nights of the northern winters. In 1649 and 1650, weakened by deadly illnesses and internal conflict, the Huron were mercilessly attacked by the Iroquois and driven from their homeland.

Around 1648, having trapped all the beaver in their own streams, the Iroquois had pushed into Huronia in search of new territory for trapping and hunting. In the ensuing battles, the Iroquois, who had acquired guns from the Dutch along the Hudson River, were better armed than the Huron. By the spring of 1649, having suffered a number of bloody defeats, the Huron abandoned their villages. Some were killed by war parties; many were adopted by the Iroquois who needed to strengthen their numbers. Those who did not starve to death sought refuge with neighboring peoples.

Many Huron joined the Petun, who shared a similar language and culture. They lived just west of Huronia along the southern shore of Georgian Bay, but they too were driven out by the Iroquois, who feared that they would take over the fur trade. For the next half-century the eight hundred survivors, mostly the Petun (also called the Tionontsti and sometimes the Tobacco) lived near Lake Superior. A band of Potawatomi living near Green Bay, Wisconsin, also sheltered one group of Huron.

In 1701, the French encouraged these few remaining Huron to settle near Fort Pontchartrain at the present site of Detroit. They began to trade with the English, who called them the Wyandot, from their original name of Wendat. They migrated over what are now the states of Michigan, Ohio, Wisconsin, and Illinois. During this time, the Wyandot took part in battles in the Great Lakes region of the United States. In 1763, they joined Pontiac's great alliance of native peoples against the British, who planned to occupy the formerly French-controlled area. They later fought alongside the British against the American colonists during the Revolutionary War and against the young United States in the War of 1812. Thereafter, they continued to face European settlement in both Canada and the United States. A few descendants still live around Detroit, but most eventually migrated to Oklahoma and now make their home on the Wyandotte Reservation.

In Canada, about three hundred Christianized Hurons survived the winter of 1649–1650 on Gahendoe Island, now Christian Island, off the coast of Huronia. The following summer they settled under French protection on the Ile d'Orléans near Quebec City and six years later moved to the mainland. Known as the Huron of Lorette, they were eventually granted a reserve, where they make their home

*W*ater and trees defined Wendake: Water formed its boundaries, and hard-woods towered above its interior.

today. Although they no longer speak their original language, they strive to sustain their identity as a people.

The People and the Land

For several hundred years, the Huron lived among the forests and lakes near the shores of Georgian Bay. The region, which could be easily crossed by foot in three or four days, was bounded on the east

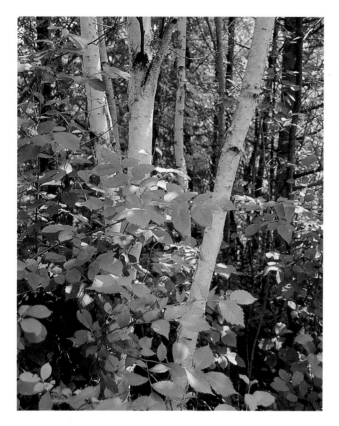

The Huron used wood to make many objects, including canoes, which they shaped from sheets of birch bark.

by Lake Simcoe, on the west by Nottawasaga Bay, and on the north by Matchedash Bay. These three magnificent bodies of water, along with rivers and marshes to the south, formed natural boundaries for Wendake.

Small lakes were scattered throughout much of this territory. The largest of these—now Cranberry Lake, Orr Lake, and Bass Lake—lay near its southern edge. Running cold and clear, streams and rivers laced the forests and fields, emptying into the shimmering lakes. The Huron briskly paddled their canoes throughout this territory and along the shores of Georgian Bay to trade corn with the French and

Algonquians, and to make war against the Iroquois and other enemies. Much of Wendake was enveloped by the bay's long, curving shoreline of shifting sands and rocks worn by the waves over thousands of years. Here, the huge expanse of water was broken only by an island, seemingly floating above the waves, or by fragments of pine-studded cliffs piercing its surface.

In stunning contrast, much of the interior was distinguished by the canopy of hardwoods—primarily maple, beech, and oak—that blanketed much of the region, blending with occasional stands of white birch, which provided bark for canoes. There were also basswood, ash, and elm, with which the Huron sheathed their longhouses. White pines sprung up in clearings, and other evergreens thrived in the moist, low ground. Cedars, which the Huron also used in building longhouses, took root in the many swamps that dotted the land.

Wendake abounded in wildlife: bear, deer, wolf, coyote, fox, wolverine, and lynx. There were also beaver, otter, muskrats, porcupines, raccoons, fishers, woodchucks, rabbits, weasels, and mink, which the Huron hunted or trapped. The marshes and lakes also teemed with fish and fowl, especially ducks and geese—the flocks were so large they often blackened the skies—as well as trumpeter swans. The Huron hunted deer for their meat and hides. They also relished the greasy flesh of bear. They could trap just about any animal, but they often traded with the Algonquian, exchanging corn and food stores for dried meat and fish. In later years, they traded beaver pelts to the French in exchange for European goods.

Like other American Indians, the Huron lived according to the cycle of the seasons. In the spring, the sap began to rise in the maple trees. They tapped the trees and boiled down the sap to make crumbly brown maple sugar. However, the Huron were primarily farmers. To the south lay rich soils, but the Huron preferred the less fertile but loose soils in their territory. Although trees had to be cleared for fields, the sandy loam was easily worked with stone tools. When the soil had thawed, they dug with sticks and planted their corn, beans, and squash, which they called the three sisters, as well as sunflowers. In early summer, they gathered berries, and in the long, dry months of July and August, as ears of corn ripened on their stalks, they gathered wild blueberries growing thick on bushes in the forest shade.

In the autumn, as the foliage turned red, yellow, and orange, the corn leaves and stalks faded to tan, the squash matured, drying beans rattled in their shells, and the sunflowers began to nod their heads. Women harvested these crops and gathered nuts before the first arctic winds swept down. Through the short days of the long winter, the snows grew deep. The rivers and lakes froze and seemingly vanished under the drifts. People settled around the orange glow of their fires, trudging short distances in snowshoes to hunt deer or to fish through the ice of a nearby lake. They also pulled toboggans and sleds over the snow. Both game and fish could be scarce during the hard winters, but the Huron had ample stores of corn and dried meat.

Whatever the season, people sustained themselves from the forests and fields, as well as the lakes and rivers, scarcely harming the

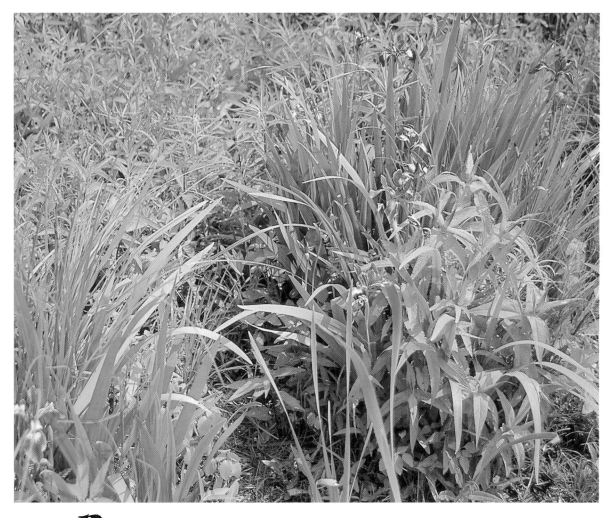

During the brief months of summer warmth, wildflowers sprang up in the marshes and meadows of Wendake.

landscape around them. The land and water belonged to no one. It was the home of their ancestors, the place where they lived, and where they trusted their children and grandchildren would make their home.

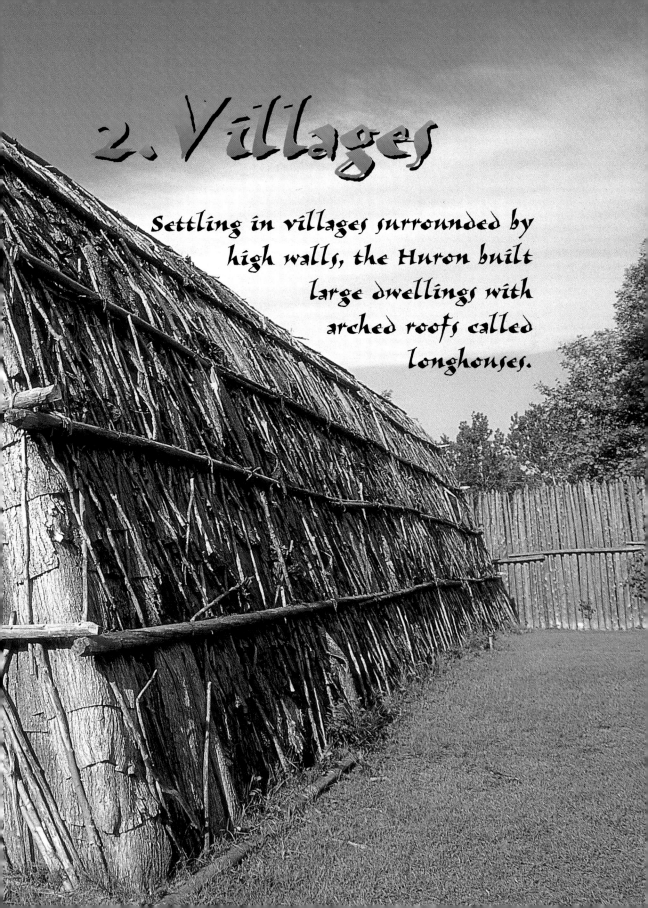

2. Villages

Settling in villages surrounded by high walls, the Huron built large dwellings with arched roofs called longhouses.

THE HURON CAREFULLY LOCATED THEIR VILLAGES NEAR WATER AND TILLABLE soil. They did not live directly on the shore of Georgian Bay because of its poor soil and strong northwesterly winds. They chose inland sites on elevated land, preferably a bluff, near streams or freshwater springs. Villages also had to be near forests for wood and building materials.

The Huron fortified many of their villages with walls, or palisades. To make the walls, men first sharpened the ends of cedar or pine logs and then placed the logs side by side in trenches, the sharp points thrusting upward. They lashed the logs together with

Men climbed ladders to these wooden scaffolds, which served as lookout posts on the inside walls of the village.

This entrance winds through a maze intended to confuse enemies attacking the village.

saplings and piled soil against the base to form a sturdy barricade. To make the single entrance, they overlapped the ends of the walls slightly, so that anyone entering or leaving the village had to turn a corner. This slowed enemies who tried to invade the village. Instead of a gate or door, the entrance was protected by wooden bars. Inside the wall the men built lookout towers and platforms reached by wooden ladders. If an attack was anticipated, they stacked rocks on the platforms to throw down on their enemies and stockpiled jars of water to put out any fires.

Within the palisade, there might be as many as forty longhouses, standing in rows, just a few feet apart, all facing northeast away from the prevailing winds. The village had a sweat lodge and a wigwam for the shaman, or medicine man. There were also storage pits and drying racks for animal hides, as well as workplaces for grinding corn, making pottery, and repairing canoes.

Longhouses

Depending on the season and the activity, the Huron lived in different types of buildings, the most common being the longhouse. About ninety to one hundred feet long and twenty to thirty feet wide, the longhouse had a rectangular base and walls that curved to form a domed roof.

Once the longhouse frame was completed, men attached sheets of elm bark to make waterproof walls and a roof.

*T*he finished longhouse was tall, allowing smoke to rise and drift through holes in the roof.

To build a longhouse, the men first constructed a wooden structure by lashing poles together. They sheathed the framework with sheets of elm or cedar bark tied down with saplings and wooden strips. Longhouses had no windows—only a low doorway at each end and holes in the roof to allow the bluish gray smoke from the cooking fires to drift out. There was usually a porch at the entrance where wood and food were stored. Inside there was a row of shallow fire pits, each about twenty feet apart. Each fire pit served two families.

The Huron built raised platforms along each side of the long-house. During the winter, people slept on the floor near the warmth of the fires and stored their goods on the platforms. During the summer, they slept outside or bunked on the wide shelves cushioned with animal hides. They hung carved wooden masks, snowshoes, weapons, and other belongings on the posts and inside walls. Otherwise they furnished their longhouses simply, with bark or husk floor mats, clay pots, baskets, and hollow logs in which corn was stored.

A single longhouse might shelter ten or more families. Usually, with as many as six members in each family, thirty-six to forty people lived in each longhouse. Weathering downpours and blizzards, as well as baking sun, a longhouse lasted about eight to twelve years.

People slept and stored their belongings on platforms raised above the earthen floor of the longhouse.

Rebuilding the longhouse was usually a cooperative effort in which people from other villages gathered to help.

Families and Clans

Clans, as well as families, formed the social structure in every village. Huron society was based on a system of eight extended families, or clans: Turtle, Deer, Wolf, Hawk, Bear, Porcupine, Beaver, and Snake. Clans owned the cornfields and the longhouses. Each family had a place within the longhouse, yet people also had to cooperate and work together as clans. Extended families included aunts and uncles and grandparents. Known as *yentiokwa*, the clans shaped the day-to-day governance of villages and tribes. All the people in a clan considered themselves related, even if they belonged to different Huron nations. People remained members of their clan for life, and all the children grew up as brothers and sisters. A large clan might occupy several longhouses in the village, and each clan was represented in the four nations. Since members considered themselves related to their kin in other nations, a strong bond existed among all Huron.

Each clan was led by a male chief. However, elders, known as clan mothers, commanded respect and were often consulted in decisions. Huron society was also matrilineal, which means people traced their descent—in both family and clan—through a female ancestor. A man was born into his mother's clan. When he grew up and married, he remained a member of his clan, but his children became part of their mother's clan. Managing the household was the exclusive domain of

*E*xtended families lived together sharing household chores within the longhouse.

the women. The clan mother directed farming and the other daily tasks shared by the women in the village. Revered for her wisdom and experiences, she also helped settle disputes within the longhouse.

The Huron League

The Huron were organized into four nations, or tribes, which constituted the Huron League. Although they shared a common language and hunting grounds, each of the four tribes lived in its own territory and governed through its own council. Each nation also followed its own customs and traced its own distinctive history. Living next to each other in fortified villages, the nations kept peace among themselves and went to war together. Around the Huron League, other Iroquoian peoples made their home: the Petun, Neutral, Iroquois, and others. Algonquian tribes were also scattered near the land of the Huron.

Huron government was based on the clans. Clan members within each village selected the chiefs who represented them in councils. Each of the eighteen to twenty-four villages in the League was governed by two separate councils. Made up of all the war chiefs and proven warriors of each clan group, the war council met in the longhouse of the most distinguished leader. Daily affairs, such as hunting, fishing, farming, defense, religion, and ceremonies, were discussed by a civil council. This council was led by a chief who was respected for his wisdom and skill as an orator. Older men, usually at least thirty years old, could attend and speak at this council.

Council members discussed matters at length, listening carefully to opposing viewpoints until everyone could agree on a decision. Any man who wanted to speak was allowed to do so. Individual clans could refuse to take part in an attack on an enemy or other action with which they disagreed. The councils lacked the authority to carry out decisions so they tried to arrive at a consensus, or general agreement.

Each tribe, or nation, was represented by a council of the head chiefs from each of the clans. These clan chiefs met in the tribal council at least once a year. Any chief of a clan could request a tribal council when an issue arose that went beyond the interests of his village. Messengers traveled to each village to announce the meeting, and the chiefs came together. After an exchange of greetings and occasionally gifts, the chiefs seated themselves by village. The chief who had called the meeting then laid the matter before the council in the form of a request for advice. The discussion was highly ritualized. Each speaker first summarized all the previous arguments to assure himself and everyone else that all had been clearly understood. As with village councils, the chiefs strived to reach a decision through consensus.

At least once a year councils of the four nations of the confederacy were held to renew and strengthen the bonds of friendship, as well as to decide how to deal with enemies. Each village sent clan chiefs, with one serving as spokesman and the others as advisors. The chiefs were seated according to clan and village. Conducted in the same manner as the tribal councils, the chiefs discussed matters con-

The people of each village sent leaders to represent them in tribal councils held within the safety of the village walls several times a year.

cerning the confederacy, but no decision was binding. The Huron League served primarily as a defensive alliance. Because of the long deliberations and emphasis on general agreement, the confederacy was seldom truly unified. Tribes could not be forced to take part in a war or defend a village. When their very survival was threatened in the 1640s, the Huron League could not respond promptly and decisively to the intensive onslaughts of the Iroquois.

3. Lifeways

As shown in this illustration by Ivan Kocsis, the Huron often smoked from a sacred pipe when consulting the spirits in matters of daily life.

As they walked along paths in the forests and paddled down the rivers, the Huron lived in harmony with the universe. As they worked in cornfields and fished in lakes, they respected the many spirits that dwelled around them. People understood themselves and their place in the world through a knowledge of daily tasks and divine powers. With no written language, they relied upon their remarkable memories to insure that the lessons of the earth flowed from one generation to another. Their way of life was recounted through stories and renewed through a complex system of religious beliefs. It is how they as individuals, families, clans, and tribes came to understand the wonder of birth, the trials of youth, and the joys of marriage, as well as the journey toward old age and death. This awareness was passed on whenever a mother placed her newborn in a cradleboard, a man taught his son to make a bow, a woman showed her daughter how to plant corn, and an old man spoke to a group of children gathered around him.

Cycle of Life

The Huron viewed themselves as one with the animals, the plants, and the earth itself—as well as the sun and the stars in the skies above them. They counted the days, months, and years by the cycle of the moon. In the spring and summer, the men left the village to trade and wage war while the women tended their green fields. During the autumn, the women gathered wild fruits and hemp in the forests while the men left again, setting up camps and fishing in the rivers and lakes. Later in the season, the men hunted until the winter

This young woman re-creates the Huron way of life at Sainte Marie among the Hurons, an historical village in Ontario.

snows deepened around them, after which families came together again, settling around the warm fires in their longhouses. As recounted in *Jesuit Relations*, their life was shaped by "the seasons of the year by the wild beasts, the fish, the birds, and the vegetation." Just as their daily life followed the seasons, so did their view of themselves as belonging to families and clans. There were many beliefs and rituals honoring the cycle of life at birth, coming-of-age, marriage, old age, and death.

Birth. The Huron rejoiced at the birth of a child, especially a girl who could potentially increase the number of people in the village. Yet parents desired both girls and boys because children were needed to help support them in old age and defend them against enemies.

There were also superstitions regarding pregnancy. It was believed that a woman heavy with child could bring either good or bad luck. Her pregnancy might prevent her husband from finding game. If the woman looked at an animal being stalked by her husband, it would

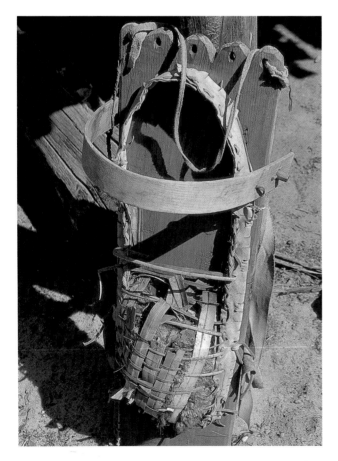

Like many native peoples, the Huron bundled their babies safely in cradleboards.

get away. If she ate with people, they would become ill. If she entered the dwelling of a sick person, the condition would worsen. Yet by her very presence she could aid in the removal of an arrow.

When a woman was about to give birth, a corner of the longhouse was partitioned with animal skins. Sometimes, an old woman served as midwife, but experienced women gave birth by themselves and seldom rested after having a baby. A woman might be carrying a load of wood from the forest or be hoeing in a cornfield when she went into labor. She would rise to her feet immediately after giving birth, and once the baby was placed in a cradleboard, she would resume her work. To prove her courage and set a good example for others, the woman did not cry out during labor—although many women died during childbirth.

Sometimes, the mother made her baby swallow grease or oil shortly after birth to insure good health. With a fish bone, she then pierced the newborn's ears, placing a feather quill in the opening. Later, she hung beads from the lobes and around the baby's neck. The Huron kept a supply of available names, those which were not being used by another person in the village. Perhaps the baby would be given a name with great meaning, such as *yocoisse* (wind), *sondaqua* (eagle), or *taihy* (tree).

Wrapped in furs or skins, the baby was placed in a cradleboard decorated with paintings and strings of beads. Soft down from a reed was used as a diaper, with an opening left in the swaddling through which the baby could make water. During the day, the mother carried the cradleboard on her back or propped it up in the longhouse or outside so her baby could watch her as she worked. During the night, the baby slept naked between the mother and father.

The mother breast-fed her baby for two to three years. While the baby was still nursing, she began to feed it bits of meat that she had chewed.

childhood. The Huron deeply loved their children and rarely disciplined them. Although allowed a great deal of freedom, children were encouraged through praise and scolding to contribute to the good of the community. Expected to be tough as well, they were scantily clothed, even in winter, to insure sturdy bodies in later life. From an early age, children were given chores around the longhouse. Young boys and girls helped weed the fields and chase birds away from the ripening corn.

As they grew up, boys learned to become skillful with bows and arrows and with spears and other weapons. They also competed in many games, such as snow snake in which they slid a curved stick as far as possible over the snow. These games helped them to build the skills as well as the strong friendships they would need as warriors and hunters. They also learned to make tools and birch bark canoes, as well as longhouses.

Mothers placed a stick in the hands of their young daughters so they might learn how to pound corn from an early age. Girls fetched water and firewood, helped cook meals, and cared for younger brothers and sisters. Following the example of their mothers and the other women in the longhouse, they learned to do household chores,

As shown in this painting by Ivan Kocsis, Huron mothers taught their daughters to become hardworking and productive.

tend crops, tan deerskins, shape clay pots, and weave baskets, some of the many skills they would need when they had a family of their own.

Coming-of-Age. When a girl had her first menstrual period she cooked her food separately in a little pot—as she would whenever she had her period again. The young woman was then considered ready to have a lover or to be married. The Huron did not discourage women from entering into relationships outside of marriage.

At puberty, a young man sometimes went on a vision quest. Venturing alone into the forest, he fasted and drank only water for as long as sixteen days in the hope that his guardian spirit would appear to him. The spirit would help him choose the right path in life. Throughout a man's life, these spirits often reappeared in dreams to offer advice. During times of danger, a man also appealed to his guardian spirit for help.

Marriage. When a man wished to marry a woman, he painted his face and put on his finest ornaments. He presented her with gifts such as a wampum necklace, bracelet, chain, earrings, or a beaver robe. If she accepted the presents, he slept with her for three or four nights. If the couple liked each other and the family consented to the marriage, they held a feast in honor of the couple. The father announced the marriage and if there were no objections, there was a feast. Everyone ate stew made of dog, bear, moose, deer meat, or fish. The couple was considered married when the feast ended.

Many young men did not have wives, or *aténonha*, but simply lived with companions known as *asqua*. Whether married or not, men and women were free to have relations with others in the village. If an unmarried woman became pregnant, her lovers came together, each claiming to be the father, and she simply chose the lover she liked best to be her husband. If a married couple did not get along,

Throughout his life, a man called upon his guardian spirit to guide him through the challenges of hunting and warfare.

they were free to leave each other. Although divorce was very common, it happened less frequently when the husband and wife had children.

Death. When a person died, friends and family lamented the loss. The deceased lay on a mat within the walls of the village, and speeches were made in his or her honor. After three days, the people held a feast in which the soul of the deceased took part. Gifts were lavished on the deceased, his family, and those who had arranged the funeral. The body was then placed on a scaffold about ten feet above

Like other Iroquoian people, the Huron often placed their dead on scaffolds, along with tools and weapons of importance during the person's life.

the ground, along with food, tools, and other belongings needed on the journey to the land of the spirits. If the person had drowned or frozen to death the body was burned. Babies less than a month old were buried near a path in hopes that their spirit would rise and enter the womb of a woman passing by.

People mourned for ten days, but the spouse of the deceased grieved for one year. During this time, they could not remarry or take part in any feasts. Every eight to twelve years, the entire village held a funeral ceremony known as the Feast of the Dead. The women recovered the bones of any relatives who had died in the previous decade. They scraped the bones clean and wrapped them in furs, after which there were several days of feasting and gift-giving. People told stories about their departed relatives, after which the bones, along with personal belongings, were buried in a large pit.

The Huron believed a person had two souls. After death, one floated near the body until it was released at the Feast of the Dead. This soul could be reborn in a name-giving ceremony. The other soul journeyed along a path toward the setting sun and the village of the dead. The soul had to pass a rock in the land of the Petun, where the *Oscotarach*, or head-piercer, drew out the brains. The soul next had to traverse a log over a turbulent river guarded by a vicious dog. After many months, the soul finally arrived at the village of the dead, which was much like that of the living. The souls of children and the very old who could not make the arduous journey went to another village, where they tended abandoned cornfields.

Gathering and Gardening

During much of their early history, the Huron wandered the northern forests and provided for themselves through hunting and gathering. Later, they learned the art of farming and gradually settled in villages. They grew corn and began to cultivate beans, squash, and sunflowers. Individuals and families claimed plots of land near the village, but these fields could not be inherited or sold. The land belonged to them only as long as they worked it.

When new ground had to be cleared, groups of men first chopped down small trees with stone axes. Some of the branches were used as

This historical engraving shows Huron women cultivating corn in fields cleared in the forest near their village.

firewood and building materials. The remaining brush was allowed to dry for a while. Then it was heaped around the stumps and burned, the ashes returning some nutrients to the soil. The men girdled, or cut a swath of bark, around the trunks of trees too large to cut down. Sap could no longer flow up the trunk and the trees died, dropping their leaves and allowing sunlight to reach the ground. Clearing the ground was arduous work; several years were required to carve a new field from the dense forest. The women planted around the stumps of the large trees until they decayed and the men could break them apart. To clear old fields that had not been farmed for a number of years, the

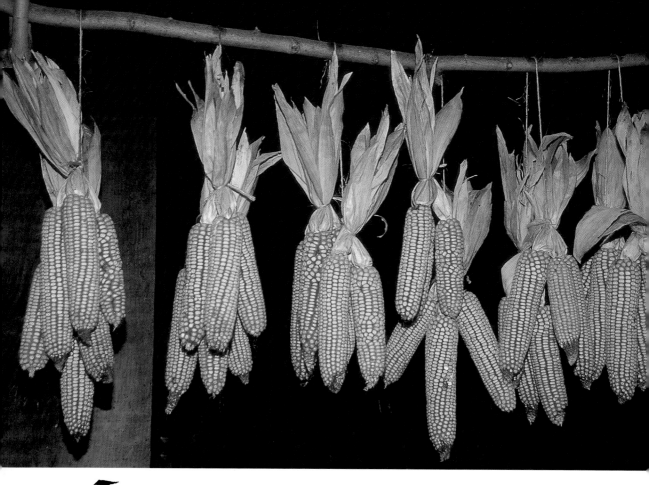

*T*he Huron stored corn and other crops in bins or underground pits.
Sometimes corn was hung from the longhouse rafters.

men simply cut down and burned off any brush that had sprouted
since the land was last cultivated. The Huron eventually cleared and
farmed all the land around their villages.

Once the men had prepared the fields, their work there was done
for the season—the women were responsible for the long months of
planting, tending, and harvesting the crops. In the spring, they
selected the best corn kernels for seeds and soaked them in water.
With wooden spades, they scraped the soil into small mounds, or

corn hills. With digging sticks, they made small holes in the mounds, dropped in as many as ten kernels, and covered them. As the clumps of corn plants sprouted, they scraped more soil around the roots. When the corn was several inches tall, women planted beans and squash in some of these hills. The vines of the beans wound up the corn stalks, and the broad leaves of the squash kept the weeds down. Women also planted sunflowers, usually in separate fields. Occasionally, men grew tobacco in small patches near their long-houses, but most often they traded for this sacred plant. They used tobacco in rituals—through the rising smoke they communicated with the spirits—or they simply enjoyed a good smoke.

Over the warm summer months, the women weeded and watered their fields—the very survival of the village depended on their bringing in a good crop. The Huron feared a late frost in the spring and an early autumn frost and a drought during the growing season. They often sought the help of spirits or called upon a medicine man who could influence the weather. Children helped the women vigilantly guard the fields from a host of hungry creatures, especially marauding raccoons and flocks of blackbirds. In late August, as the colors turned in the surrounding forests, they harvested their crops. Sliced and dried, squash kept well for several months, as did the beans, which hardened in their pods. However, corn was by far the most important crop grown by the Huron. Some of the corn was shelled and stored in bins or underground pits. The husks pulled back, ears were also hung in bunches from the rafters, away from mice.

When they weren't working in their cornfields or longhouses, women harvested many wild foods and plant materials. They picked strawberries, raspberries, blackberries, blueberries, and wild cherries, as each came into season. The berries were eaten fresh or dried for the winter and used to flavor corn soups and breads. Women also gathered wild grapes, dug bulrush roots, and collected acorns and walnuts from the forest floor. They found mussels along the lakeshore and caught turtles in the nearby marshes. In the late summer, they stripped basswood bark, which they boiled, shredded, and made into rope. After the winter storms had knocked dead limbs from the trees, they hauled huge amounts of the wood to the village where it was needed to cook meals and warm the longhouses.

Hunting and Fishing

While the women tended the crops and gathered foods, the men hunted and fished. In the spring, they caught sturgeon, pike, catfish, sucker, and walleye in the streams and shallow waters along the lakeshore. Sometimes they fished with bone hooks, but their lines often broke, so they relied on nets, wooden spears with barbed bone points, and underwater traps made of wooden slats, called weirs. Poised quietly on the bank or in their birch bark canoes, they speared larger fish. The men scooped up small, schooling fish in dip nets or caught them in weirs. They placed the weirs near the mouths of creeks along spawning runs. The fish would swim into the wide opening and become trapped as the weir gradually narrowed. In the autumn, groups of men journeyed to the islands of Georgian Bay for

*I*n this illustration by Ivan Kocsis, men wade into the water to spear fish while others gather on the bank to dry their catch.

whitefish, lake trout, and lake herring. During this month-long fishing season, they set up bark cabins and lived in camps away from the village. In the evening, they stretched long seine nets with wooden floats and stone weights in the water. In the morning, they drew the seine together, trapping large numbers of fish. During the bitterly cold winter, they occasionally netted fish through holes chopped in the ice.

The men hunted deer, moose, bear, rabbits, muskrats, wood-chucks, and beavers, as well as ducks, geese, turkeys, and other birds. The only taboo was eating the flesh of the crow. The Huron killed beavers for their meat and valuable fur with snares, arrows, and clubs. By the 1630s, most of the beaver were gone from Wendake. Dogs were occasionally sacrificed during feasts or eaten during the lean winter months. However, bear and especially deer were the most common sources of meat. Groups of men used spe-cially trained dogs to stalk bears, whose meat was prepared for feasts. They hunted deer with bow and arrow, or caught the fleet-footed creatures in snares and traps. However, a village most often organized a communal hunt, or drive, in which a large number of people, including women and children, spread out in the woods. They drove the frightened deer over river bluffs or into V-shaped fences where the animals were cornered and easily shot with bow and arrow. Deer were hunted for both their meat and their hides, which were made into clothing or traded with the French and other native peoples.

Making Meals

Women cooked all the meals for their families, usually over the fire pit in the longhouse. They boiled soups and stews in pots and roasted meat and fish. Corn, which comprised about three-quarters of the Huron diet, was included in most meals. Dried and shelled, the kernels were ground between two stones or pounded in a hollowed-

*W*omen ground their corn between two stones or with a wooden pole in a
hollowed-out log.

out log with a wooden pole about seven feet long. The coarse yellow
meal was added to soups and made into unleavened breads. Women
formed the dough into small cakes, which they wrapped in corn
husks and baked under hot ashes.

Sagamité, (sa-GA-mi-tay) a cornmeal soup, was a favorite among
the Huron. Slices of fish, meat, or squash were often tossed into the

pot of sagamité. At feasts, a thick corn soup was usually served. A special soup was made from roasted corn kernels mixed with beans and leindohy, immature ears of corn fermented for several months in stagnant water. Leindohy was considered a delicacy. Beans, which were dried and stored in bark or wooden containers, were also eaten, along with squash—especially in the late summer and autumn. The Huron garnished dishes with sunflower oil and rubbed the oil on their bodies and in their hair. Fruits, nuts, and maple syrup were sometimes added to soups and stews. Especially during times of famine, acorns were eaten, but only after they had been boiled repeatedly to remove the bitter taste.

During the hunting season, meat was plentiful but still not a major part of Huron meals. Meat was smoked and mainly served during feasts. Fish was eaten more often. It was sometimes fresh but usually had been smoked or dried where it had been caught. Larger whitefish were sometimes boiled and the oil skimmed off and stored in gourds. One fish known as *einchataon* (possibly catfish) was hung to dry high in the rafters where smoke lingered in the longhouse. Occasionally fish were gutted, but often they were cooked whole with bones, scales, and entrails intact.

Except during feasts and times of abundance, the Huron ate twice a day—early in the morning and in the evening. However, a cooking pot was always simmering over the fire, and people could eat whenever they were hungry. They did not wash their hands, but if they were greasy, they simply wiped them on a nearby dog.

Sagamité

Sagamité, which means water or warm gruel, was a traditional cornmeal soup, the staple of the Huron diet. To make the soup, women boiled cornmeal in clay pots—about one part cornmeal to nine parts water. Sometimes, women tossed chunks of meat or fish into the cooking pot as well.

Over time, the name sagamité came to apply to any number of soups, stews, and other Huron dishes. Today, a sagamité recipe with deer meat and kidney beans is served as a dinner meal on the Wendake reserve near Quebec. Here is a basic recipe without meat that you might try as a hot breakfast cereal.

Ingredients

1 ½ cups cornmeal	½ tablespoon salt
5 cups of water	1 cup of blueberries
1 tablespoon of butter	Sugar
	Milk

Mix the cornmeal with one cup of cold water, then add four cups of boiling water, salt, and butter. Cook in the top pan of a double boiler for about 25 minutes or until the mixture has thickened.

Place equal amounts of the sagamité in bowls and sprinkle with blueberries or other fruit. Serve with sugar and milk. Serves four or more people.

Clothing and Jewelry

Women made all the clothing for their families, mostly from soft buckskin, moose hides, or beaver pelts. Many of the hides came from their own hunting, but some were acquired through trade. Buckskin clothing was usually fringed and often painted with red or brown designs. Robes were trimmed with porcupine quills dyed bright red.

During the warm months, men wore only a buckskin breechcloth and moccasins made from deer, beaver, or bear. As winter set in, they donned leggings and long-sleeved shirts and wrapped themselves in beaver cloaks. Many men also wore a fire pouch in which they carried tobacco, pipes, charms, and other belongings. Pipes were especially prized, and men never came to a meeting without having a smoke. Men dyed their hair and wore it in a variety of styles—mostly long but also short or in what is known today as a Mohawk. They often stuck feathers in their hair or wrapped an eel or snakeskin around their head.

In the summer, women wore only a knee-length buckskin skirt and moccasins. In cold weather, they draped a mantle over their shoulders and added a fur robe. Women wore their hair long, with one braid hanging down the back and tied with a leather thong. For dances, they oiled and dyed their hair, then wrapped a tuft with an eel skin band.

Wampum—tubelike beads made from seashells—was pierced and strung to create jewelry. Both men and women adorned themselves with highly prized wampum bracelets and necklaces. Women also wore earrings and belts of wampum, porcupine quills, or bone.

This Huron man with hair cropped close on top is adorned with earrings and necklaces made from bones, shells, and glass beads.

As shown in this illustration by Ivan Kocsis, women often pulled their hair back and wore necklaces, earrings, and other jewelry,

Both men and women often painted, oiled, and greased their bodies and hair. They mixed minerals or dyes from plants with sunflower oil or animal fat and painted designs on their faces and bodies—red and black were favorite colors, but they also used green and violet.

Handicrafts

The Huron did not make handicrafts for trade but only those needed in the longhouse and village. And when villagers packed up and moved, they often left their household goods behind.

Along with tending children, raising crops, gathering firewood, cooking meals, and managing the longhouse, women crafted those objects essential to their lives. They scraped and softened deer and other animals skin into supple leather for clothing, game bags, and tobacco pouches. They wove mats of reeds and corn leaves, which they placed over doors and on sleeping platforms in the longhouse. Women also wove baskets from reeds and birch bark and sewed pieces of birch bark together to shape cups and bowls. Women also wove fibers into small textiles, including scarves, collars, and bracelets worn by both men and women.

Women made all the household pottery. First, they dried and crushed the clay dug from a riverbank. Next they mixed in a little powdered rock to strengthen the clay, then added a small amount of water. After shaping a mound of clay into a ball, they punched a hole in the middle with their fist. With their fingers and a small wooden paddle, they gradually formed the pot into a globe, with a narrow opening and low rim. To harden the clay, the finished pot was dried in the sun and baked in an open fire. Women made pots in many sizes—from a few inches to a foot or more in diameter. Cooking pots were made in three sizes, for individuals, families, and village feasts. Small diagonal, vertical, or horizontal lines were scratched near the lip of the pots. When cold, the pots could not hold water for very long before the clay began to soften. However, they could be used for cooking over a fire.

Smoking pipes were also made from clay—most likely by the men. They shaped the moist clay around a knot of grass, which burned away when the pipe was fired. A small number of highly skilled potters specialized in fashioning pipes. They took greater care in making pipes than pots—better clay was used and the pipe was more evenly fired. Before firing the pipe, potters sometimes rubbed grease over the object to blacken the surface. With round or flared bowls, pipes were often decorated with human or animal figures. Pipes were highly prized, especially those made by the most talented potters, and often used as barter in a trade.

During the summer, men also built or repaired the longhouses and palisades. Through this work, along with the clearing of fields, men pushed back the forest and created a reasonably safe area around the village. Men also used the time between the busy fishing and hunting seasons to make canoes or repair old ones. Many of these tasks were undertaken cooperatively, often by all the able-bodied men in the village. To construct a canoe, they carefully formed the ribs from white cedar so the vessel would be balanced and float

Women were skilled primarily in two useful handicrafts—weaving and pottery making. They wove reeds into mats and baskets of many sizes and styles, and they shaped soft clay into cooking pots.

gracefully in the water. They sheathed this frame with birch bark cut in the spring when the bark was easily peeled from the tree. They sewed the birch bark pieces together with cords and joined them to the frame by weaving a strip of cord along the edge of the canoe. To make the canoe watertight, they boiled pine sap and sealed the seams with the sticky pitch, which hardened into a tough resin.

During the winter, men kept busy in the warmth of the long-house. They skillfully wove light, yet sturdy fishnets. They carved wooden bowls, spoons, and ladles. Occasionally, they made ladles from antlers, using the shapes of the points to suggest a duck in flight. The men fashioned snowshoes and sleds and made clubs and bows and arrows for hunting and warfare. They made points for their

The seams of this birch bark canoe have been sealed with pitch to make the vessel watertight.

Men fashioned snowshoes for trudging through the forests to hunt game throughout the long winter.

arrows from chert, a kind of flint for which they traded. Men also made spear points, awls, and needles from bone. From granite and other hard stones, they chipped the heads for axes and adzes.

Sometimes, they carved pipes from stone and made ornaments, such as tube-shaped beads, from bird bones. They also worked seashells into disk-shaped beads and whittled combs and little amulets from bone.

Warfare

Like the forest and the clearing, warfare and peace were two opposing forces that had to be balanced within Huron society. So, the village and the tribe had separate chiefs and councils for waging war against hostile peoples and maintaining friendly relations with others. When trading with neighbors, the Huron forgave slights and injuries, but warriors confronted their enemies beyond the clearing with great bravery—and no mercy.

For hundreds of years before the French ventured into the upper reaches of North America, the Huron, as well as other Iroquoians and the Algonquians, had been engaged in raids against hostile villages. The Huron fought the Petuns, possibly the Neutrals, and the five tribes of the Iroquois League, especially the Senecas. In fact, the war with the Iroquois had gone on for half a century. The Huron had also established a network of trade alliances with the Algonquians of Ontario and Quebec and other tribes in the region. These tribes, in turn, fought or traded among themselves or with others, resulting in a complex web of relationships—either hostile or friendly—among all the peoples between the St. Lawrence River and the western Great Lakes.

Like other Iroquoian peoples, the Huron went to war primarily for blood revenge and prestige. In the 1640s, as the fur trade began to change their lifeways, the Huron started to fight other tribes over hunting and trapping territories. Each year, leaders who had proven themselves in battle planned and organized war parties—usually in the late spring or summer. The warriors always gathered in secret for fear of spies within their villages. They dreaded the possibility of informers in their midst and often exiled visitors from the village or even tortured and killed them. Huron chiefs befriended members of neutral tribes and even recruited some of their enemies as spies in the hope they would warn them of any attack on their villages.

Before war was waged, a great feast was held and the war party excitedly set off for enemy country in birch bark canoes. Five to six hundred warriors took part in these raids; in later years even larger war parties were formed. Each warrior sheathed his chest, arms, and legs in armor made of tightly laced sticks. Armed with war clubs, knives, and bows and arrows, he carried either a long, cedar bark shield or a small disk of tough, boiled leather into battle. Around his head, the warrior wore a circular ornament of red moose hair and his finest jewelry. It was believed that if he was pursued, he could throw down these valuables and the enemy would stop to gather them. Each warrior also brought along a bag of roasted cornmeal—enough to last two months, if necessary.

The warriors might lay siege to an Iroquois village for as long as a week. Once they had killed and captured a number of people, they

Among the weapons of the Huron were the bow and arrow and the war club, which warriors used in close combat with their enemies.

retreated to Wendake. The following year, the Iroquois might retaliate in similar fashion. Most often, however, when the party reached enemy territory, the warriors broke into groups of five or six and scattered in the woods around the villages. They ambushed small, isolated groups of people as they fished or worked in the fields, killing or capturing men, women, and children. Some daring warriors slipped into the village at night and terrorized people as they slept. If possible, warriors brought back their enemies' heads or scalps to dry and hang in the longhouse during wartime.

However, a captive was the greatest prize; warriors sought to bring back as many as possible. Some captives, especially women and children, were adopted by families who had lost a relative in war. Most, however, were submitted to a merciless ordeal and then killed. Not only the warriors but women and children thirsted for revenge. Everyone took part in an enemy's highly ritualized torture and slow death. Captives were told to sing during their agony. If they cried out or otherwise failed to display great courage, they and their tribe would be shamed. During the ritual, torturers became increasingly fierce and cruel as they tried to break their victims. Similarly, when Huron warriors were captured and tortured, they were expected to be unflinching—to stand as a symbol of their people.

Travel and Trade

Men journeyed throughout Huronia on foot or by canoe to hunt, trade, and wage war. During the winter, they wore snowshoes, or *agnonra*, strung with animal gut for trudging through the deep snows. The Huron also fashioned a sled, or arocha, with boards of white cedar for hauling goods over the ice. For river travel, men favored small, swift, light canoes paddled by one or two men. Swinging the canoe over his shoulders, a man could easily tote this light craft around rapids or along portages from one stream to another. The Huron relied on large canoes, up to thirty feet in length, to carry people and goods over great distances. They paddled these canoes over the broad waters of Georgian Bay and the many lakes around Wendake. Since the birch bark sheathing of these canoes was easily damaged, the men always paddled within sight of the shore.

The Huron often traveled to trade with other tribes—they rarely bartered among themselves. They won respect and approval in the village by acquiring wealth and generously sharing it with others. They bestowed gifts at name-giving ceremonies, burials, and during feasts and festivals. They scorned anyone who hoarded goods—a stingy person could be accused of witchcraft and banished.

They traded only with those tribes with whom they had established a peace agreement and a military alliance. Because of long-standing hostilities with the Iroquois, the Huron never bartered with these tribes. In negotiating to trade furs with Champlain, the Huron insisted that the French first prove their friendship by participating in raids against the Iroquois. To maintain good relations with their allies, the Huron made every effort to prevent insult or injury to members of allied tribes, especially murder, which would ignite bloody warfare between tribes. Clans and villages kept a treasury of goods from which they made large payments to the family of a

Huronia *was the crossroads of an extensive network of trading routes.*

murder victim. A chief could also dip into the treasury to arrange treaties and exchange prisoners, the size of the payment depending on how highly the Huron valued trade with that partner.

The Huron established far-reaching trade routes from their base at the southern tip of Georgian Bay—north to James Bay, east to the St.

Lawrence River, south to the Susquehanna River in present-day Pennsylvania, and west to Lake Michigan. The man who discovered a new route held rights as its owner, as did his family members or "those who held his name." His family shared in his trade, while unrelated people had to offer gifts to the rights holder. Those who owned the trade routes often amassed great wealth and became prominent chiefs in their villages. Anyone caught encroaching on a trade route was severely punished. However, if he safely made it back to the village, he would not be harmed. Similarly, the Huron ruthlessly guarded their trade routes from the Petuns, Neutrals, and other tribes outside the confederacy. Anyone who wished to cross their territory had to first seek permission—a violation led to war.

Men often traded for the sheer adventure. As in warfare, they proved their courage by embarking on a dangerous journey. The Huron loved games of chance and sometimes acquired goods for gambling. However, they traded primarily for desirable objects that could be ritually given away, thereby enhancing their prestige within the village. Among the most highly valued goods were shells for making wampum that had made their way from far-off Chesapeake Bay, chert from the neighboring Petuns and Neutrals, native copper from the shores of Lake Superior, and tobacco. In their cold climate, the Huron could grow little tobacco, so they obtained as much of the sacred plant as possible from the Petuns and Neutrals, and later from the French.

The Huron acquired black squirrel pelts from the Neutrals, made them into cloaks, and traded them to the Algonquians. From the

Ottawa the Huron obtained dried berries, mats, fish, and furs in exchange for wampum, nets, and pigments. In addition, the Huron traded pots to Ojibwe living on the eastern shore of Lake Superior and cornmeal to the northern tribes. Many traders were active in this network, which only expanded with the fur trade. The French clearly admired the bargaining skills of the Huron and eagerly formed a partnership that grew into an international trade, especially in beaver pelts. At the height of the fur trade, as many as three hundred Huron regularly traveled to the St. Lawrence River, and one year seven hundred men made the journey.

4.Beliefs

As shown in this illustration by Ivan Kocsis, medicine men were called upon to heal the sick and injured.

THE HURONS BELIEVED THAT EVERYTHING ON EARTH, WHETHER LIVING trees or inanimate rocks, had a spirit. The more powerful of these spirits, which included the sun, the moon, and the sky, were known as *oki*. The sky was an especially vital force, being the source of the weather and the waves on the sea, both of which were divine. The Hurons made offerings of tobacco—or sacrificed captives—to please and honor the sky. Certain men, such as shamans (medicine men) and great warriors, were considered oki, as were charms that had proved to be effective.

Because animals had spirits, the Huron also honored them. They never burned their bones or fed them to their dogs. While fishing,

This shaman wears amulets to ward off illness and evil spirits.

they prayed and offered tobacco to the spirit of the waters. Some spirits were seen as human, or partly so. *Ondoutaehte*, the spirit of war, could be a dwarf or an old woman. *Onditachiaé*, the spirit of thunder, lightning, and rain, might appear in the form of a human or a wild turkey.

After the sky, the most powerful spirits were Aataentsic, for the moon, and her son (or grandson in some stories) Youskeha, the sun. Here is a story about these two great spirits.

"Aataentsic and Youskeha"

Aataentsic was the moon, and Youskeha was the sun. Both governed the world. Youskeha was responsible for the living—the plants, animals, and people. It was also Youskeha who brought sunshine and rain when needed and other things that helped the people. In contrast, Aataentsic ruled the land of souls and brought death to people.

Although gods, Aataentsic and Youskeha lived as other people but with such an abundance of corn that they had many feasts. Though they dwelled far away, they also often came to the feasts and festivals in the villages of the Huron. At one of these joyful occasions, Aataentsic was badly abused and insulted. Youskeha blamed a horned oki named *Tehonrressanden*, but later everyone learned that it was actually Youskeha who had abused Aataentsic—his own mother.

Despite his misdeed, Youskeha was still respected by the Huron, while Aataentsic remained resentful of Youskeha who brought much good to the world. At one time, all the water was held under the armpit of a frog. Youskeha slit the armpit, and water flowed over the earth, forming much-needed rivers, lakes, and seas. From the wise turtle, Youskeha learned to make fire, and he generously shared this knowledge with the people.

Similarly, Youskeha once kept all the animals of the world in a great cavern. But he wanted them to multiply and spread over the land, so one day he freed the creatures. He shot each in the foot with an arrow—all except the wolf who nimbly dodged the arrow. Because of Youskeha's generous act, the forests abounded in game, and the Huron had good hunting. However, the men have always had difficulty hunting the elusive wolf.

Youskeha also influenced the harvests of corn. If his spirit was glimpsed in the fields, thin as a skeleton and carrying a stunted ear of corn, the people knew they would not have a good crop that year. Yet if he was seen to be in good health, the Huron knew they would harvest much corn.

While Youskeha cared for the living, Ataentsic often undid his helpful deeds. One year, she brought a plague to the villages, and as she journeyed through the longhouses, the people asked her, "Why do you make us die?"

She wrongly blamed her son. "It is because Youskeha is angry at men. They only make war and kill each other. To punish them for their cruelty, he has decided to make them all die." However, when he became old, Youskeha always renewed himself in a moment and became a young man again. He never died. Through the ages the two powerful spirits of Youskeha and Aataentsic battled, seemingly as opposite as life and death yet one never really separate from the other.

Healing and Dreams

The Hurons did not build special lodges for religious ceremonies. Like the Iroquois, however, they had a number of healing

Members of religious societies may have worn masks—an idea borrowed from the Iroquois. Some were made of corn husks or carved from wood.

societies. The members of these groups either inherited their powers, received them in a dream, or obtained them through recovery from an illness.

The members of some healing societies crawled around the patient in animal skins or danced in straw masks. Known as *Awataerohi*, the most prominent society held the Dance of Fire to heal the afflicted. They called upon powerful spirits as they chewed hot coals and sometimes spat them on the patient. Although the system of beliefs within the community was quite complex, religion was also a highly personal matter. Whether shamans, warriors, or traders, individuals were empowered through a vision or by acquiring a powerful companion spirit.

The Huron had an intricate system of beliefs about preventing illness and curing the sick. They believed that illness came not only from natural causes but also from evil spirits and unfulfilled wishes. People suffering physical illnesses or injuries were treated by a shaman with herbal remedies. Wild sarsaparilla was given for wounds and Indian turnip roots for head colds. If the patient did not get better, the Huron believed the sickness must have a supernatural cause.

A shaman, or *ontetsan*, treated people afflicted by both illness of the body and spirit through magic, feasts, dances, and spells. He usually removed one or more offensive objects from the person's body—a tuft of hair, an animal claw, or perhaps a feather. He touched or shook the patient, then symbolically displayed the object. It was sometimes believed that a witch had cast a spell over the person. So the shaman tried to find the witch. If the witch could not remove the spell, he or she might be executed, if the chief or council so ordered.

If the patient was suffering from unfulfilled wishes, the medicine man interpreted his or her dreams. Then he asked the patient's relatives to help fulfill these unsatisfied desires. Every winter, many people in the village took part in a three-day festival known as *ononhouaroia*, or "the upsetting of the brain." Most often, the event was triggered by the illness of a well-known person. A group ran through the village, loudly shouting, acting crazy, and telling the inhabitants of each longhouse, "We have dreamed." They didn't reveal what had been dreamed, only hinted through riddles until they received the desired objects. This ritual not only provided a reason for gift-giving, the Huron believed that it helped to protect the well-being of everyone in the village. At the end of the festival the participants went into the woods to "cast out their madness" in hopes that the ill person would get better.

Festivals and Dances

The Huron loved to host feasts at which guests sang, danced, and ate heartily. Usually held during the late autumn, winter, or early spring, these gatherings were an important way to strengthen friendships and to improve one's social status within the village. The host was respected because he freely shared his wealth and good fortune. There were four kinds of feasts: *enditeuhwa*, to offer thanksgiving; *awataerohi*, to cure a sick person; *athataion*, for a dying person to say farewell to his close friends; and *atouronta ochien*, to sing in preparation for war, to honor a man who wished to be renowned, or to give the name of a deceased chief to another person. At some gatherings, known as *anondahoin*, only tobacco was smoked. People arrived at feasts in their finest clothing and ornaments. They carefully styled their hair and often painted their faces and bodies. Inside the longhouse, the guests sat on mats or cedar boughs spread on the ground or on the platforms.

Shaking tortoise-shell rattles, two chiefs led the singing. They stood in the midst of the dancers, who formed a loose oval around them. The feast might last all day or several days. Food was served in the morning and afternoon when the host announced, *Nequarre*! ("the kettle has boiled"). The guests joyfully responded, *Ho*!, and struck the ground or platform. Along with singing, dancing, and eating, these gatherings were enlivened with games and spirited contests.

Games and Gambling

The Huron loved to play games and gamble. Good luck in gambling was believed to come from supernatural forces. Whether between individuals or teams of villagers and neighbors, no contest was ever held without a lively wager, and the stakes were often high. Men were known to gamble away everything they owned—even their clothing. One man had to cut off his little finger, which he had lost on a bet. Sometimes, men were so ashamed of their losses that they could not face their families and killed themselves. Gambling also led to angry fights and even murder.

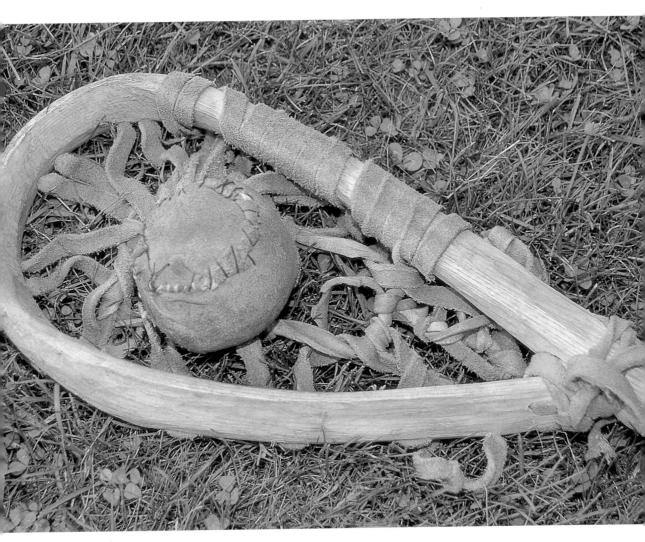

Among the most popular games was stickball, an early version of lacrosse, which men played with rackets.

The three favorite games were stickball, the dish game, and *aescara*. Known by most native peoples around the Great Lakes, these games were played to cure sickness and prevent disaster. The Huron

*P*eople attached feathers to corncobs to make darts, which they tossed into a hoop laid on the ground.

also competed at stickball to bring good weather or to honor a dead player. Played with a ball and sticks in a field near the village, this early version of lacrosse was a rough game, a kind of war game with frequent injuries in which young men proved their courage. The dish game was played with five or six fruit stones or small pottery disks painted black on one side and white or yellow on the other. Sitting in a circle, people took turns putting the stones in a wooden bowl and then striking the bowl on the ground. One side won when all the stones fell out with the same color facing up. Women also played the dish game, but they held the stones in their hands and dropped them on an animal hide stretched on the ground. Little is known about *aescara*, except that one player held three or four hundred white reeds. Another player snatched a handful of reeds and then guessed how many reeds his opponent still held.

Like feasts and dances, games were part of the *onderha*, the foundation of social life among the Huron.

5. Changing Ways

The Huron way
of life changed
dramatically as the
trade in beaver pelts and
other furs became an
international
business.

WHEN THEY FIRST MET SAMUEL DE CHAMPLAIN, THE FOUNDER OF NEW France which later became Canada, the lives of the Huron began to change forever. Leaders met with the French and soon established a lucrative trading partnership, exchanging beaver pelts for European goods, including cloth, glass beads, knives, and kettles. At the time, beaver hats were the height of fashion in Europe and demand for the pelts was great. Because of their geographic location and experience as traders, the Huron were ideally located to serve as middlemen in what became known as the Great Huron Trade Circle. The Huron obtained European goods from the French, which they in turn

Over time, many people converted to Christianity, which led to a bitter division within Huron society.

traded, along with their own corn to their neighbors, including the Petun, Neutral, Ottawa, Algonquin, and Nipissing for beaver pelts. Beaver were plentiful where these native people lived. Then, the Hurons returned to their homes and traded the beaver pelts to the French.

However, the Hurons came to depend upon metal tools and household goods, including pots, skillets, and kettles. They also began to rely on guns as weapons. They soon lost the knowledge and skills to make clay pottery and buckskin clothing, as well as their own tools and weapons. The demand for furs was also so intense that they had less time to grow food for themselves, let alone surplus corn, beans, and squash to trade with their northern and western neighbors and the French.

The French also sent missionaries among the Huron. Known as Black Robes, the Jesuits attempted to convert native people to Christianity. Because the Huron had settled in villages, the Jesuits believed that they would be easier to approach and convert than the nomadic tribes. However, the deeply personal beliefs of the Hurons differed markedly from those of Christianity. For many years, they resisted efforts to force them to abandon their traditional beliefs. Then, between 1635 and 1640, smallpox and measles epidemics swept through Huron villages, reducing the population to just 10,000 people. Unable to understand the devastation or find a cure, many Huron turned to Christianity as a last refuge. Others blamed the missionaries for bringing the disease to their villages, and conflict arose between these two factions.

Eventually, the Black Robes were able to influence and change the Huron way of life. Here is a song by Father Jean de Brébeuf (1593–1649) that blends traditional Huron life with the Christmas story. Composed by Father Brébeuf in the Huron language in the 1600s, the song was passed down since the 1600s through generations of converted Hurons before being translated into French and English.

The Huron Carol

'Twas in the moon of the wintertime
When all the birds had fled,
That mighty Gitchi Manitou sent
angel choirs instead;
Before their light the stars grew dim
and wond'ring hunters heard the hymn:
"Jesus, your King, is born,
Jesus is born. In excelsis gloria!"

Within a lodge of broken bark
The tender babe was found.
A ragged robe of rabbit skin
Enwrapped His beauty 'round;
And as the hunter braves drew nigh
The angel song rang loud and high:
"Jesus, your King, is born,
Jesus is born. In excelsis gloria!"

*H*uron beliefs came to blend traditional and Christian beliefs as expressed in this painting of the Nativity by Ivan Kocsis.

The earliest moon of wintertime
Is not so round and fair
As the ring of glory
On the helpless infant there.
The chiefs from far before Him knelt
With gifts of fox and beaver pelt.
   "Jesus, your King, is born,
   Jesus is born. In excelsis gloria!"

O children of the forest free.
O sons of Manitou.
The Holy Child of earth and heaven
is born today for you.
Come kneel before the radiant Boy
Who brings you beauty, peace, and joy.
   "Jesus, your King, is born,
   Jesus is born. In excelsis gloria!"

Weakened by disease and internal conflict, the Huron were attacked in the early 1640s by the members of the Iroquois League to the south—Mohawk, Oneida, Onondaga, Seneca, and Cayuga tribes. The Iroquois had established a similar trading partnership with the Dutch of New Amsterdam (later New York), and they wanted to trade with the same northern tribes with whom the Hurons had been exchanging beaver pelts. Armed with Dutch guns, Seneca warriors attacked villages in 1648 and a year later, devastated by war, disease,

*I*n this painting by William Bent Berczy, Hurons are shown leaving their home near Amherstburg, Canada, for a hunting expedition.

and starvation, the Huron abandoned their territory. Many, including most of the Tahontaenrat clan, merged with the Onondaga and Seneca tribes, which had also lost many people.

Others, whose descendants are still known Huron, or Wendat, migrated to the island of Gahoendoe in Georgian Bay. However, there was little farmland on the island and the largely Christian group was encouraged by Jesuit missionaries to move to Quebec and settle among the French in 1650. The next year about four hundred Huron left Quebec and settled on Ile d'Orléans in the St. Lawrence River. Their population grew to five or six hundred within the next five years, but seventy-one people were killed in a Mohawk attack in 1656, after which the Huron sought peace with the Iroquois League. The Attignawantan clan joined the Mohawks, strengthening their declining population, and the Arendahronon became part of the Onondaga. The Onondaga, however, betrayed the agreement and killed all the Huron men and took the women as children as captives.

*P*aul Tahourencht (François Xavier Picard) became the principal chief of the Hurons at Lorette, Quebec.

About two hundred Attignawantan stayed in Quebec. For the next forty years they sought a home, moving to Beauport on the St. Lawrence River in 1667 and then to Côte St.-Michel. In 1673, their population having grown to three hundred people, they migrated to Ancienne Lorette, where they lived for twenty-four years. As their population grew, they had to move again, in 1697. This time they moved to Jeune Lorette, eight miles north of the city of Quebec, where they became known as the Huron of Lorette. The sandy soil there was not suitable for agriculture and when the Huron lost hunting and fishing territory in 1701, they began to support themselves by making traditional crafts—moccasins, snowshoes, and canoes—and selling them in nearby Quebec. The Huron received additional lands, including 1,352 acres known as Quarante Arpents in 1772 and 9,600 acres known as Cabane d'Automne in 1851. They leased and later sold the parcels of land so they could continue to specialize in traditional handicrafts. With a population of more than 2,500 people, the Hurons still operate their businesses on the Wendake Reserve, although many have adopted a French-Canadian style of life.

After the Iroquois wars, another group of Hurons moved southwest, just twenty-six miles away, to live among the Petun and the Neutral, their former trading partners. But they enjoyed only a few years of peace. Toward the end of 1649, the Iroquois again attacked and drove them from their new homes. They became wanderers—through what is now Michigan, Wisconsin, Ohio, and Illinois. They first settled on the island of Michilimackinac (mish-ullee-MACK-uh-nack), now known as Mackinac Island, and then Huron Island, which was later named Rock Island, near Green Bay, and then farther west in Wisconsin. They subsequently moved near Detroit and then northern Ohio. Along the way, the Huron-Petun traded and hunted with other mostly Algonquian-speaking peoples, as well as fought against other tribes. While in Detroit, the Huron-Petuns became trading partners with the British, who came to refer to them as the Wyandot.

However, most Wyandot continued to ally themselves with the French, especially since the British were allied with the Iroquois. When the French lost the French and Indian War (1754–1763) and surrendered their territory in North America, the Wyandot continued to fight the British. Led by Pontiac, a great Ottawa chief, an alliance of tribes that included the Wyandot attacked Detroit, Fort Pitt, and Sandusky. During the American Revolution, however, the Wyandot sided with the British. After the American Revolution ended in 1783, they faced a new enemy—Americans pushing westward. In the early to mid-1800s, the Wyandot settled in Ohio and east of the Mississippi River. However, by 1843, they had sold all these lands and moved to Indian Territory in the fork of the Kansas and Missouri Rivers in what is now Wyandotte County, Kansas. They purchased land there from the Delaware, or Lenape, people.

In 1855, a Wyandot delegation negotiated a treaty with the United States government that provided for allotment, or distribution, of their lands to tribal members. Each individual received a parcel of the land that had once belonged to the group. But the tribe

A *group of people donned their finest dress for this photograph taken at Village de Hurons at Loretteville.*

These Hurons paused in their work on the Seneca Reserve in Ontario—their new home.

as a whole lost its identity. The Wyandot who received land became United States citizens, but surrendered their tribal membership. The Wyandot also suffered prejudice from settlers and were often cheated out of their land. They fell into deep poverty and in 1867 many people moved to the northeastern part of Indian Territory in present-day Oklahoma where the Senecas, their former enemies, gave them refuge. The Senecas eventually granted over 20,000 acres of land to the Wyandot on the north side of their reservation.

The United States government upheld this agreement with the Senecas and this small group of Wyandot, numbering about 110 people, were soon joined by others who had lost their land in Kansas. They formed a government with annual meetings and the election of first and second chiefs and council members. On the eve of Oklahoma statehood in 1907, Wyandot lands were again allotted with the surplus lands to be sold to settlers. This time, some tribal members were not even included in the allotment process, although the United States Congress had promised to purchase lands for them elsewhere. Some Wyandot went to Ohio, and others returned to Canada where they were again known as Hurons and where they live to this day.

In 1937, the Wyandot reorganized under the Oklahoma Indian Welfare Act of 1936. However, in 1956, the United States embarked upon another termination process, which not only ended federal assistance but threatened the very existence of the Oklahoma tribes, including the Wyandot, with the loss of their land. The Wyandot were allowed to retain their governments, but without land they had no way to remain together as a people. By the late 1960s, it became obvious that the termination plan was a disaster, as native peoples not only lost land, but a sense of community and identity as a people.

Today, the Wyandot have regained their status as a federally recognized tribe, and they have maintained their capital at Wyandotte, Oklahoma. However, their population had dropped from between 20,000 to 45,000 in the mid-1600s to fewer than 1,000 people in 1944. In the mid-1990s, one Wyandot chief was believed to be the last known speaker of their native language in the United States, although vigorous efforts are now being undertaken to revive the language.

Huron Language

The Huron spoke a dialect of the Iroquoian language family. The Jesuits reported that the Attignawantan and Petun spoke the same language, but the Attignawantan and Tahontaenrat spoke slightly different dialects. Because of their prominence in trade in the early 1600s, the language of the Huron was adopted by the French and a number of Algonquian-speaking peoples who lived around the Great Lakes. However, when the Huron were devastated and dispersed, their language and culture became threatened. It is believed that the last fluent speaker of the language in Canada died in 1912. Today, most Hurons in Canada speak French while the Wyandots living the United States speak English.

The following words and phrases are drawn from *An Ethnography of the Huron Indians, 1615–1649* by Elisabeth Tooker. The original sources are the *Jesuit Relations* and the accounts of Recollect friar Gabriel Sagard-Théobat. Pronunciations are not at present available.

Words and phrases about daily life

agochin	a feast
agnonha	iron person; Huron word for the French
aiendawasti	a polite person
cachia otindion	You are very clever.
chay	good day
chieske	What do I know?
ho, ho, ho	a joyful greeting
ho, ho, ho, outoécti	many thanks
ondayee ihaton onennoncwat	That is what my heart says to me, that is what my appetite desires.
oniondechouten	Such is the custom of our country.
téondion (or tescaondion)	You have no sense.
yo eiouahaoua	Come, put on the kettle.

Spiritual life

arondiuhanne (or ahondiuoyissa)	words for a medicine man: "You are people who understand high and supernatural matters."
endionrra	the soul that thinks and deliberates
gonennoncwal	the soul in so far as it bears affection to any object
khiondhecwi	the soul that gives life to one's body
oki andaérandi	like a spirit; the soul possessed of reason

Animals

ahonque	Canada goose
ahouyoche	trout
anarisqua	wolf
angyahouiche	turtle
ausquoy	caribou
hixrahon	sturgeon
horhey	swan
ondathra	muskrat
ondettontaque	wild turkey

oraquan	crow
scangaresse	skunk
sconoton	deer
sondaqua	eagle
sondareinta	moose
soruissan	pike
taron	duck
tintian	woodpecker
tioointsiq	snake
tochingo	great blue heron
tsoutaye	beaver

Fruits and berries

hahique	small fruits in general
ohentaqué	blueberries
poires	pears
tichionte	strawberries
toca	cranberries
tonestes	plums

6. New Ways

Today, many Hurons earn a living by making canoes and snowshoes on their reserve in Canada.

AT ITS HEIGHT, THE HURON CONFEDERACY WAS AT LEAST 20,000 STRONG, although some estimates run as high as 45,000. Today nearly all the Hurons in Canada live on the Wendake Reserve near the city of Quebec. About 3,000 Huron-Petuns, known as Wyandots or Wyandottes, are scattered throughout the United States, including about 350 people living on tribal lands in Wyandotte, Oklahoma.

Today, with more than 3,000 people, the Wyandot of Oklahoma no longer have a reservation. They live scattered around the United States, but still own 188 acres near the town of Wyandotte. About 350 people live on this land, and another 500 people make their home elsewhere in the state of Oklahoma. Those living in or near the community of Wyandotte are led by their own Wyandot Council. Consisting of a chief, second chief, and four councillors, each elected to a two-year term, the group manages the Wyandot Tribal Center and oversees federal programs. The council holds monthly meetings at which anyone in the community can bring up concerns. There is also an annual meeting in which new members of the council are chosen. Council members are largely concerned with improving the education of Wyandot children and providing better housing for their people, as well as greater employment opportunities. An important goal of tribal leaders is to create greater economic self-sufficiency for individuals living in the community. The Wyandot are also working to improve health care, notably the prevention and treatment of diabetes and heart disease, both of which are prevalent among their population. They had established a health clinic staffed

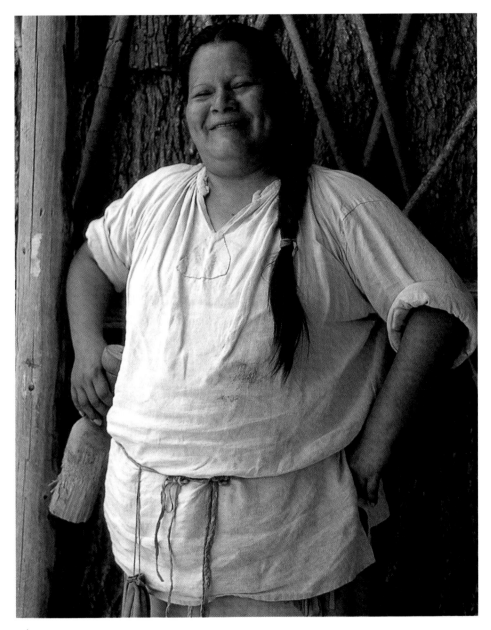

Women re-create the traditional Huron way of life at Sainte Marie among the Huron in Midland, Ontario.

by two doctors. The next closest facility is the Indian Health Service Hospital—five hundred miles away in Claremont, Oklahoma.

During the first half of the twentieth century, the community of Wendake, the reserve near Quebec where the Huron of Lorette make their home, steadily dwindled—both in population and size. People left the reserve, and leaders sold much of the land. The Canadian government also confiscated some of the land for parks and the national railroad until the Huron had just twenty-six acres in the late 1960s. In 1968, Huron leaders negotiated with the Canadian government, which returned native lands and the reserve was enlarged to over 165 acres. The Huron also embarked on a number of successful business ventures, and today the people of the Wendake Reserve enjoy one of the highest standards of living of native peoples in Canada. Many people own their own stores or small businesses while others commute to jobs in Quebec and other towns. Several people have entered professions as doctors, authors, musicians, and artists. However, many people have devoted themselves to traditional handicrafts for which the people at Wendake are widely acclaimed. During the 1990s they produced 3,000 canoes and 50,000 pairs of snowshoes each year. Today, people live in modern houses along shady streets amid thriving enterprises. Children attend Huron Elementary School from grades one through four, then travel to nearby schools in Loretteville or Quebec.

The reserve is governed by the Huron National Council, consisting of five members elected to two-year terms. Chosen as chief councillor, one member presides over all meetings. The council manages community issues, including health care, and programs funded by the Canadian government. Today, about one thousand Huron live at Wendake and around the same number live off the reserve in Canada and the United States. Despite their prosperity, the Huron continue to petition the Canadian government for the return of a portion of their ancestral lands. Many people attend Nôtre-Dame-de-Lorette, a Catholic church built at Wendake hundreds of years ago. However, the Huron have also committed themselves to reviving traditional ways of life. Efforts are being made at the elementary school to teach children about the history and culture of their ancestors, including instruction in the Huron language.

Today, there are more than 2,500 Huron in Canada and about 4,000 Wyandot in the United States. Although the Huron and Wyandot have little contact with each other today, they share a common history. As descendants of one of the greatest confederacies in North America, they have struggled to overcome the devastating changes brought about by the French, British, and Americans, including widespread death from warfare and disease. Like other native peoples, the Huron and Wyandot are proud of their heritage and determined to thrive in the larger societies of the United States and Canada. Despite massive upheaval over the past four centuries, they have struggled to maintain the thread of traditional culture that gives them identity as a people, whether in Oklahoma or Canada. Looking toward the future, they are also striving to build prosperous lives for themselves amid the political structure and economy of the contemporary world.

More About

the Huron

Time Line

1500s Four tribes unite to form the Huron League

1609 The Hurons encounter the French, most likely explorer Samuel de Champlain, the founder of New France

1626 The first Jesuits, accompanied by Recollect friars, enter Huronia

1649 The Huron must abandon their homeland because of the wars with the Iroquois League

1697 After wandering for half a century, some Hurons settle in Jeune Lorette, north of Quebec, which becomes the Wendake Reserve

1843 The remnants of one Huron group, known as Wyandot or Wyandotte, arrive in Kansas

1855 The Wyandotte Tribe cedes its land in Kansas City, Kansas, to the United States, except the "portion of land now enclosed and used as a public burying ground," which is today known as the Huron Cemetery

1867 The Wyandot who choose not to become citizens of the United States are granted a reserve of approximately 20,000 acres in what is now Oklahoma

1937 The Wyandot adopt a constitution under the Oklahoma Indian Welfare Act and become known as the Wyandotte Tribe of Oklahoma

1956 The United States moves to terminate the Wyandotte Tribe and demands that all tribal land be sold

1968 The Canadian government expands the Wendake Reserve to more than 165 acres

1977 When petitioned to reinstate the Wyandotte as a tribe, Congress determines that the Wyandotte was still legally considered a tribe

Notable People

Adario (Kondiaronk, Sastaretsi, Gaspar Soiaga, Souoias, Le Rat, The Rat) (about 1650–1701), a leader, diplomat, and speaker, was born a Petun, but his people joined the Hurons after the Iroquois invaded their territory in the mid-1600s. He grew up to become a great chief during the first of the French and Indian Wars. He become a skilled diplomat, especially in playing the French against the Iroquois who were allied with the British. Adario also spoke eloquently in defense of his people's rights.

In 1688, with arms furnished by the French, he led a war party against the Iroquois. On the way, he was told that an Iroquois peace delegation was headed to Montreal. Adario ambushed and captured the Iroquois, telling them that the French had ordered the attack. To show his goodwill, he freed the captives, keeping one hostage to replace one of his men killed in battle. Adario then journeyed to Michilimackinac where the commandant had not yet heard that the Iroquois wished to have peace. So, he ordered the captive to be executed. When he returned to his village, Adario released another Iroquois captured in a previous battle, sending the warrior home with the message that the French had killed the other captive despite the Hurons' efforts to spare him. On August 25, 1689, the furious Iroquois killed hundreds of people in attacks on Montreal and other French settlements along the St. Lawrence River. Adario managed to remain friendly with the French while convincing the Iroquois that he was also sympathetic to them.

In later years, Adario converted to Christianity. He died while heading a peace delegation in Montreal in 1701. The French buried him in a cemetery there with full military honors.

Ahatsistari (Eustache Ahatsisteari) (active mid-1600s), war leader, headed two victories against the Iroquois in 1641–1642, early in the wars with their neighbors to the south. In one battle, he led fifty warriors against three hundred Iroquois; in the other, the warriors fought in canoes on

Lake Ontario. Not long afterward, a band of Mohawks attacked a French and Huron war party and captured Ahatsistari. He was briefly held prisoner, then killed.

Seven years later, in March 1649, the five tribes of the Iroquois League swept into Huron territory north of Lake Ontario, drove them from their villages, and took over the region.

Deganawida (Deganawidah, Dekanawida, Dekanawidah, Dekanahwidah; The Heavenly Messenger) (active 1500s), Huron spiritual leader, is believed to have been born near present-day Kingston, Ontario, in the early to mid-1500s, one of seven brothers. According to legend, his mother foresaw in a vision that he would cause the Huron people to be destroyed. So, she tried to drown him three times in a nearby river.

When he grew up, Deganawida crossed Lake Ontario, presumably in a stone canoe, and met Hiawatha, a Mohawk warrior, in what is now New York State. The two men envisioned a union of the five tribes, which came to be known as the Iroquois League. It is believed that Deganawida, who had a speech impediment, was the visionary and Hiawatha was the spokesman who journeyed among the Cayuga, Mohawk, Oneida, Onondaga, and Seneca. After he had founded the league, planted the tree of life, and written the Great Law, Deganawida became a Pine Tree Sachem, a leader chosen by merit instead of heredity. Other versions of the story recount that Deganawida departed in his stone canoe, vowing to return if the alliance was ever threatened.

In 1649, the Iroquois attacked and defeated the Huron, fulfilling the sad prophecy of Deganawida's mother.

Dunquat (Dunquad, Daunghquat, Half-King) (active late 1700s), leader, was a Wyandot, the descendants of the Hurons who migrated to present-day Ohio. He became a leader of allied bands of Wyandot, Shawnee, Ojibwe, and Ottawa warriors that allied with the British during the American Revolution. Dunquat led a series of attacks against American settlements

A group of Huron chiefs posed in formal ceremonial dress for this photograph at Lorette, Quebec.

west of the Allegheny Mountains. Serving as a peacemaker among tribes, he also protected the Christianized Moravian Delawares from an attack by another faction. After the Revolutionary War, Dunquat allied with Little Turtle, a Miami chief, and continued to resist westward movement of American settlers. In 1795, he signed the Treaty of Fort Greenville along with Little Turtle.

Tarhe (Crane, Le Chef Grue, Monsieur Grue) (1742–1818), medicine man, was born at Detroit and became a leader among the Wyandot. He allied with Cornstalk, a Shawnee chief, against settlers at Point Pleasant in Lord Dunmore's War of 1774. Then he fought with Little Turtle at Fallen

Timbers in 1790–1794. Tarhe played a pivotal role in negotiating the Treaty of Fort Greenville of 1795 and thereafter became an American ally. A friend of Shawnee chief Catahecassa, he opposed Tecumseh's advocacy of resistance against westward expansion. He allied with the Americans during the War of 1812 and fought at the Battle of the Thames in 1813. He died at Crane Town, near the present-day site of Sandusky, Ohio. Many notable people, including the Seneca chief Red Jacket, attended his funeral.

William Walker (1800–1874), interpreter, leader, was the son of a white captive, who became a chief of the Wyandots in Ohio, and his mixed-blood wife. Educated among settlers, Walker studied European languages at Kenyon College. He served as private secretary and interpreter for Lewis Cass, the governor of Michigan Territory. Later, he became a source for Henry Rowe Schoolcraft who studied native peoples of the Great Lakes region.

When his father died in 1824, Walker became chief of the Wyandots in Ohio. Opposed to removal, he fought for the best possible terms when his people were relocated to Kansas in 1842. He became the provisional governor of the Nebraska Territory in 1853, which was divided into the Kansas and Nebraska Territories the following year.

Walk-in-the-Water (Myeerah) (about 1775–about 1825), leader, came to support Tecumseh's dream of an independent nation, although he had signed peace treaties with the United States at Detroit in 1807 and 1808. During the War of 1812, he and Roundhead, another Wyandot leader, allied with the British and proved to be effective warriors. On January 22, 1813, they fought with Colonel Henry Proctor against a force of Kentuckians at Raisin River south of Detroit. On October 5, 1813, Walk-in-the-Water also took part in the Battle of the Thames, where Tecumseh was killed. After the war, Walk-in-the-Water made his home near Brownstone, Michigan.

Glossary

Algonquian Native peoples of North America who speak Algonquian languages and, in many cases, share similar customs. All the non-Iroquoian tribes in the Northeast were Algonquian, including some of the Huron's immediate neighbors—especially the Ottawa, the Nipissing, and the Algonquin. Ojibwe, Delaware, Abenaki, and Potawatomi are among the many other Algonquian tribes of North America.

Algonquin See Algonquian

birch bark A thin layer of bark from the birch tree that may be fashioned into coverings for canoes, wigwams, and useful household items.

Black Robes Name for the Jesuit missionaries who sought to convert the Hurons and other native peoples in Canada.

breechcloth A cloth or skin worn between the legs and around the hips; also breechclout.

buckskin Deer hide softened by a tanning or curing process.

clan A number of families related to a common ancestor.

confederacy A political union of related tribes, such as the Huron and the Iroquois, for warfare and trade.

fur trade A network through which native peoples exchanged animal furs, notably beaver pelts, for European goods.

Hiawatha A great Mohawk statesman, who helped found the League of the Iroquois.

Huronia The region between Georgian Bay and Lake Simcoe in Ontario that was the homeland of the Huron. Also known as Wendake.

Iroquoian The group or family of languages spoken by related tribes in eastern North America, including the Huron and the six Iroquois tribes.

Jesuit A priest in the Society of Jesus, a Roman Catholic order founded by Saint Ignatius Loyola in 1534.

longhouse A dwelling of the Huron and other Iroquoian people, consisting of a wooden framework sheathed with elm or cedar bark.

oki Supernatural powers, including the sun and sky, as well as companion spirits of individuals.

ononhouaroia A Huron ceremony, literally meaning "the upsetting of the brain," in which people guessed and tried to fulfil each other's secret dreams.

palisade A defensive wall of upright, sharpened poles surrounding a Huron village.

reservation Land set aside by the United States or Canadian government as a home for an Indian tribe; called a reserve in Canada.

sagamité Corn soup commonly eaten by the Huron.

wampum Shell beads in strings or collars used by the peoples of eastern North America as jewelry and as symbols of good faith in treaties.

Wendake The Huron homeland also known as Huronia; also, the home of the modern Huron of Lorette.

Wendat The Huron name for themselves, meaning "Islanders" or "Dwellers on a Peninsula."

Wyandot The descendants of the Huron and other tribes who moved to the Great Lakes region and then Ohio before settling in their present home in northeastern Oklahoma.

Further Information

Readings

Many fine books have been written about the Huron. Among them, the following titles were very helpful in researching and writing *The Huron*:

Barbeau, Marius. *Huron-Wyandot Traditional Narratives in Translations and Native Texts*. Ottawa: Canada Dept. of Northern Affairs and National Resources, 1960.

Encyclopedia of North American Indians. Tarrytown, NY: Marshall Cavendish, 1997.

Gros-Louis, Max. *First Among the Hurons*. Montreal: Harvest House, 1974.

Heidenreich, Conrad E. *The Huron: A Brief Ethnography*. Toronto: Dept. of Geography, York University, 1972.

Heidenreich, Conrad. *Huronia: A History and Geography of the Huron Indians, 1600-1650*. Toronto: McClelland and Stewart, 1971.

Hodge, Frederick Webb, ed. *Handbook of American Indians North of Mexico*. New York: Rowman and Littlefield, 1965.

Malinowski, Sharon, and Sheets, Anna. *The Gale Encyclopedia of Native American Tribes*. Detroit: Gale Research, 1998.

Malinowski, Sharon. *Notable Native Americans*. New York: Gale Research, 1995.

Shanks, Ralph, and Lisa Woo Shanks. *The North American Indian Travel Guide*. Petaluma, CA: Costaño Books, 1991.

Tanner, Helen Hornbeck. *Atlas of Great Lakes Indian History*. Norman: Published for the Newberry Library by the University of Oklahoma Press, 1987.

Tooker, Elisabeth. *An Ethnography of the Huron Indians, 1615–1649.* Smithsonian Institution. Bureau of American Ethnology, Bulletin 190. Washington, DC: U.S. Government Printing Office, 1964.

Trigger, Bruce G. *The Children of Aataentsic: A History of the Huron People to 1660.* Kingston, Ontario: McGill-Queen's University Press, 1987, 1976.

Trigger, Bruce G. *Handbook of North American Indians.* Northeast. Volume 15. Northeast. Washington, D.C.: Smithsonian Institution, 1978.

Trigger, Bruce G. *The Huron: Farmers of the North.* 2nd ed. Fort Worth: Holt, Rinehart and Winston, 1990, 1969.

Waldman, Carl. *Who Was Who in Native American History: Indians and Non-Indians from Early Contacts* Through 1900. New York: Facts on File, 1990.

Young people who wish to read more about the Huron will enjoy these excellent books for children, a number of which were also consulted in researching and writing *The Huron*.

Bonvillain, Nancy. *The Huron.* New York: Chelsea House, 1989.

Brébeuf, Jean de. *The Huron Carol.* Toronto: Lester & Orpen Dennys, 1990.

Doherty, Craig A. *The Huron.* Vero Beach, FL: Rourke Publications, 1994.

Kelly, Robert W. *The Huron, Corn Planters of the Eastern Woodlands.* Scarborough, Nelson Canada, 1986.

Kinietz, W. Vernon (William Vernon). *The Indians of the Western Great Lakes, 1615–1760.* Ann Arbor, MI: University of Michigan Press, 1991, 1965.

Lomask, Milton. *Saint Isaac and the Indians.* San Francisco: Ignatius Press, 1991, 1956.

Ridington, Jillian. *People of the Longhouse: How the Iroquoian Tribes Lived.* Buffalo, NY: Firefly Books, 1995, 1982.

Ross, Jane Barks. *The Magic Moccasins.* 2nd ed. Columbus, Ohio: Vimach Associates, 1985.

Schwabacher, Martin. *The Huron Indians.* New York: Chelsea Juniors, 1995.

The two stories included in this book were adapted from several sources including "Huron-Wyandot Traditional Narratives," by Marius Barbeau, published in the *National Museum of Canada Bulletin* 165 (1960); *An Ethnography of the Huron Indians, 1615–1649*, by Elisabeth Tooker; *The Huron: Farmers of the North*, by Bruce G. Trigger; and accounts in *Jesuit Relations*.

Organizations

The Huron of Lorette own and operate a thriving enterprise making canoes, snowshoes, and other fine crafts at Village des Hurons on the Wendake Reserve. The Huron Indian Village and Sainte-Marie among the Hurons are superb historical sites in Midland, Ontario. The Wyandotte have their tribal headquarters in Oklahoma.

Bande Indienne de la Nation Huronne-Wendat
145 rue Chef Aimé Romain
Village des Hurons, QC G0A 4V0
Canada
Tel: 418-843-3767

Huronia Museum & Huron Indian Village
549 Little Lake Park Road
Midland, ON L4R 4P4
Canada
Tel: 705-526-2844
Fax: 705-527-6622
E-mail: hmchin@bconnex.net
Sainte-Marie Among the Hurons

Huronia Historical Parks
Box 160
Midland, ON L4R 4K8
Canada

Tel: 705-549-8064
Fax: 705-549-4858
E-mail: hhp@hhp.on.ca

Wyandotte Tribe of Oklahoma
P. O. Box 250
Wyandotte, OK 74370
Tel: 918-678-2297
Fax: 918-678-2944

Websites

American Indians have recently assumed a great presence on the Internet. Here is just a sampling of the best and most interesting websites created by or about the Huron and other native peoples.

Huron History
http://www.dickshovel.com/hur.html

Huron/Wendat Newsletter
http://www.tdi.net/ISHGOODA/RACIAL/RACHOME.htm

Sainte-Marie Among the Hurons
http://www.saintemarieamongthehurons.on.ca

Wyandot Nation of Kansas
http://history.cc.ukans.edu/kansas/wn/wn_main.html

Wyandotte Band of Anderdon
http://www.tdi.net/ishgooda/anderdon/anderhom.htm

Wyandotte Tribe of Oklahoma
http://www.wyandottenation.com/index.html

Index

Raymond Bial

HAS PUBLISHED MORE THAN THIRTY CRITICALLY ACCLAIMED BOOKS OF PHO-tographs for children and adults. His photo-essays for children include *Corn Belt Harvest, Amish Home, Frontier Home, Shaker Home, The Underground Railroad, Portrait of a Farm Family, With Needle and Thread: A Book About Quilts, Mist Over the Mountains: Appalachia and Its People, Cajun Home,* and *Where Lincoln Walked.*

He is currently immersed in writing *Lifeways*, a series of books about Native Americans. As with his other work, Bial's deep feeling for his subjects is evident in both the text and illustrations. He travels to tribal cultural centers, photographing homes, artifacts, and surroundings and learning firsthand about the national lifeways of these peoples.

A full-time library director at a small college in Champaign, Illinois, he lives with his wife and three children in nearby Urbana.